T0197614

# Smiles for God
# from a Sunflower
# and You

Written and Illustrated by
**Delace Wofford Canada**

WestBow Press books may be ordered through booksellers or by contacting:

WestBow Press
A Division of Thomas Nelson & Zondervan
1663 Liberty Drive
Bloomington, IN 47403
www.westbowpress.com
844-714-3454

ISBN: 978-1-4497-8695-3 (sc)
ISBN: 978-1-4497-8694-6 (e)

Library of Congress Control Number: 2013903818

Print information available on the last page.

WestBow Press rev. date: 02/26/2021

WESTBOW
PRESS®
A DIVISION OF THOMAS NELSON
& ZONDERVAN

This book is dedicated to my grandchildren
and future generations as they become aware of
who they are and their purpose to be a reflection too!

Your seed is so small,
But yet you grow TALL.

Who towers
over many other flowers?

You get your name from that
which gives you strength.

Even though its distance
is far in length!

The name
is
the same
for you are a reflection,

A mirror image of God's election.

Who are YOU that shines
in a rain-shower?

Simply the....... Sunflower!

Beautiful and complex in design,

You inspire in us a worship
of God divine.

The Lord who put you together
so delicately wrought,

Out of the depths of the
earth you are brought.

Beginning as a small seed,
You sprout only as the
Creator can see.

Hidden away your journey begins,
As the warmth of the sun
and rain's moisture lends.

The necessary events for
the seed to swell,
In hopes that the root will
break out of the shell.

Out of its shell and into the
ground, The root takes hold like
an anchor sound.

As the rains continue
to water your spot,
The stalk shoots out
and you grow a lot.

Who sees you now,
as the earth takes a bow?

Really just a plant at this stage
yet, "Seed leaves" open
and nourishment is met.

Quickly new leaves
take their place,
Appearing as twins
like opposite face.

TALL and straight
it quickly ascends,
Until the crown of its glory begins.

At first a green bud
grows at the top,
But quickly
this turns into the crop.

The bud is a ball
of tightly packed petals,
Protected by bracts that
are tough as metal.

In your center is thousands
of tiny "disk florets,"
Surrounded by brilliant
bright-yellow "ray florets."

Each is a flower of its own,
Each blooms separately,
but never alone.

Green bracts now hold up
the disk quite strong,
As bright outer petals
attract insects along.

Bees, butterflies, and
others are needed,
As each floret is ready
to be seeded.

The insects do their job,
While eating nectar the
pollen they rob.

Thus cross-fertilization
will occur,
As another big flower begins its allure.

Daily it faces the sun's warming rays,
As the tiny seeds grow
for many days.

All seeds grown
the flower now fades,
Its beauty gone,
but the potential lays,
With the replica it stays,
Awaiting God's timing and
His ways.

Now brown
and
burdened down,
The flower releases
its seeds to the ground.

Passed along in each seed
which was made,
God's command
to be fruitful was laid.

Same as the sunflower,
which follows the light,
We too need to direct our sight.

In following God's Son,
Who for us salvation He won!

God desires that we reflect
His glory,
So we die to self
and become His story.

To the image of His son, Jesus,
God now leads us.

On our face,
A smile we do
trace.

For our countenance
begins to shine,
with a grateful spirit in line.

Just like the flower that
reflects the sun,
YOU too can mirror
God's only Son.

# Divine Reflections

Your seed is so small,
But yet you grow tall.
Who towers,
Over many other flowers?
You get your name from that which gives you strength,
Even though its distance is far in length.
Who are you that shines in a rain-shower?
Simply the Sunflower!
Beautiful and complex in design,
You inspire in me a worship of God divine.
The Lord who put you together so delicately wrought,
Out of the depths of the earth you are brought.
Beginning as a small seed,
You sprout only as the Creator can see.
Hidden away your journey begins,
As the warmth of the sun and rain's moisture lends.
The necessary events for the seed to swell,
In hopes that the root will break out of the shell.
Out of its shell and into the ground,
The root takes hold like an anchor sound.
As the rains continue to water your spot,
The stalk shoots out and you grow a lot.
Who sees you now, as the earth takes a bow?
You break forth through the surface and the wind says, "wow!"
Now wind, rain, and sun combine their power,
To aid in nourishing the young flower.
Really just a plant at this stage yet.
The "seed leaves" open and nourishment is met.
Soon new leaves take their place,
Appearing as twins like opposite face.
Tall and straight it quickly ascends,
Until the crown of its glory begins.
At first a green bud grows at the top,
But quickly this turns into the crop.
The bud is a ball of tightly packed petals,
Protected by bracts that are tough as metal.

In your center is thousands of tiny "disk florets,"
Surrounded by brilliant bright-yellow "ray florets."
Each is a flower of its own,
Each blooms separately, but never alone.
Green bracts now hold up the disk quite strong,
As the bright outer petals attract insects along.
Bees, butterflies, and others are needed,
As each floret is ready to be seeded.
The insects do their job,
While eating nectar the pollen they rob.
Thus cross-fertilization will occur.
As another big flower begins its allure.
Each morning at dawn the flower changes position,
Leaning toward the sun as it makes its transition.
Daily it faces the sun's warming rays,
As the tiny seeds grow for many days.
All seeds grown the flower now fades,
Its beauty gone, but the potential lays,
Within the replica it stays,
Awaiting God's timing and His ways.
Now brown and burdened down,
The flower releases its seeds to the ground.
Passed along in each seed which was made,
God's command to be fruitful was laid.
Same as the Sunflower, which follows the light,
I too need to direct my sight.
In following God's Son,
Who for us salvation He won!
God desires that we reflect His glory,
So I must die to self and become His story.
To the image of His Son, Jesus,
God now leads us.
On my face,
A smile I do trace.
For my countenance begins to shine,
With a grateful spirit in line.
Just like the flower that reflects the sun,
I too can mirror God's only Son.

Printed in the United States
By Bookmasters